MIND
MONSTERS

MIND MONSTERS

How to STOP Negative Invaders of the Mind

KEVIN GERALD

Tulsa, Oklahoma

MIND MONSTERS
© 2005 by Kevin Gerald

Published by Insight Publishing Group
8801 S. Yale, Suite 410
Tulsa, OK 74137
918-493-1718

Unless otherwise noted, all Scripture quotations are taken from the *New International Version*, © 1960, 1962, 1963, 1968, 1971, 1972, 1973, 1975, 1977, 1995 by the Lockman Foundation. Used by permission. Scripture quotations marked NKJV are taken from the Holy Bible: New King James Version, © 1979, 1980, 1982 by Thomas Nelson, Inc., publishers. Scripture quotations marked AMP are taken from The Amplified Bible, Old Testament, © 1965, 1987 by Zondervan Corporation. New Testament, © 1958, 1987 by The Lockman Foundation. Used by permission.

ISBN 1-890900-44-3
Library of Congress catalog card number:2005927443

Printed in the United States of America

Dedication

To my daughter, Jodi, who completed a fantastic career as a student athlete at Western Washington University in the spring of 2005.

Jodi, when you stepped out of your "safe world" and into the high-pressure world of collegiate athletics, none of us knew the mind monsters that awaited you. Armed with your faith and determination, you excelled as a student while earning your B.A. in business, and you became a team leader and star athlete on the basketball court. You stayed true to your dreams and were a great example of a true Christian in a liberal, secular environment.

Only your mom and I know the many mind monsters that you defeated along the way. You're a champion!

Contents

Negative Invaders of the Mind

Chapter 1

Have you ever had the wrong thing in mind? Have you ever had one of those moments when it dawned on you, "I haven't been thinking right"? It's as if a light suddenly comes on!

Then you realize your mind has been consumed with insecurity, worry, fear, anger, or other negative thoughts.

Mind monsters are the negative invaders of your mind. These invaders come and:

- steal your joy and peace
- disrupt your relationships
- take away your contentment in life

They steal your life, one day at a time.

You're not the only one dealing with mind monsters. In fact, a mind monster almost kept Joseph from marrying the mother of Jesus. When we read the story of Jesus' birth, it's easy to see how close Joseph came to messing up God's plan.

> Mind monsters are the negative invaders of your mind.

The Bible records that Mary and Joseph were engaged to be married. Back in those days, if you were engaged, you were committed; it took a divorce to become unengaged.

When Joseph found out Mary was pregnant, he knew it wasn't *his* child. He also knew Mary's penalty could be death—it was a horrible disgrace for a woman to be pregnant out of wedlock.

His decision? " *. . . he had in mind to divorce her quietly*" (Matt. 1:19).

He had in mind! Notice how his thinking had gone off course. His mind was on a completely different track than the plan of God.

An angel came along and pointed out, "Joseph, you've got the wrong thing in mind. God's got a plan going on here and you're not thinking right. You've got to get the right thing in your mind" (see Matt. 1:20-23).

If you want to live a successful Christian life, you have to take a stand against the negative invaders of your mind.

> If you want to live a successful Christian life, you have to take a stand against the negative invaders of your mind.

Have you ever awakened sad? Your mind is whining, "Oh boy, another day! Oh my, a blue Monday! A terrible Tuesday! A weird Wednesday! A tough Thursday! A frightening Friday! A stinking Saturday!"

These wayward thoughts cause you to turn on your Country-Western music and sing, "It's raining outside and it's raining inside too. I've got trouble on my mind and I don't know what to do."

What happened to *"This is the day the Lord has made; [I will] rejoice and be glad in it"* (Ps. 118:24)?

Well, it went out when sadness came in, sadness created wayward thoughts, and the mind monster of sadness is jumping around inside your mind wreaking havoc! It's saying, "Let's go claim Monday as a day of sadness. Let's go ahead and move into Tuesday and call it terrible."

The mind monster is at work and everything is sad, everything's gloomy, but there's really no reason for it to be that way.

The negative invader of your mind came in and created wayward thoughts.

God had an assignment for you that day. You were supposed to go to work happy. You were supposed to walk in and smile at the folks in the office, greeting them with good cheer.

You were supposed to let your light shine before men so they could see your good works and then honor and glorify God (see Matt. 5:16). That was God's plan before

Thoughts are like trains—they take you somewhere.

sadness—the monster—invaded your mind.

Now you're off on a completely different track, feeling bad and walking into the office with your head hanging. Your coworkers ask, "Did you have a good weekend?" (They had a party!) You're moping around, but heaven's going on!

You've just been taken over by a mind monster!

You see, thoughts are like trains—they take you somewhere. There are so many people ending up in places where they don't want to be and they're wondering how they got there.

Many times, they assume God put them there. I've heard people say, "You know, God put me in this wilderness. I'm hungry and I can't feed my kids, but God put me here."

And you know, more often than not, God's saying, "I didn't put you there. You boarded the wrong train of thought." The wrong train carries:

- thoughts of worry
- thoughts that create guilt
- thoughts that cause you to feel insecure, questioning yourself
- thoughts that bring sadness
- thoughts that cause suspicion of others' motives

- thoughts that bring doubt of God and His Word
- inaccurate assumptions

For example, have you ever met a person who assumed something about you that wasn't true?

I remember a day when I left church quickly to catch a plane for a speaking engagement. My assistant had picked up a sandwich from Subway for me because I didn't have time to eat lunch. I raced to the airport with no time to spare.

When I arrived, I jumped out of the car, hurried to the check-in counter, and said, "Is there any way you can get me on the plane? Can you get my baggage checked through? I have a speaking engagement tonight and I've got to get on this plane!"

I remember watching the attendant work slowly. I was wondering, "What's bothering him? Why is he treating me this way?"

Finally, he blurted out, "The next time you're running late to the airport, don't take the time to stop at Subway and pick up a sandwich."

Being the great man of God that I am, I recognized the mind monster of violence that jumped into my mind! Longing to leap over the counter and grab him by the neck, I saw a flash, a picture of that negative imagination.

Being the great man of God that I am, I rebuked that thought! I cast it down. I brought my thoughts into captivity and kindly responded with something like, "I really didn't get the sandwich myself, but that's okay. Would you just please let me on the airplane?"

Inaccurate assumptions strike everyone. The man at the ticket counter put two and two together and assumed that I stopped and hung out at Subway.

He concluded that he shouldn't have to rush: "This tardy customer isn't going to create an emergency for me! I've been here all day waiting for him to get here. He obviously stopped at Subway and now he wants to fire me up and get me going. I'm not hurrying for him, because I know what happened. I see the bag in his hand!"

Are you wondering, "How do I become more spiritual? How do I get closer to God?" Your spiritual life is won or lost in your mind.

Every day, you're going to be bombarded with mind monsters coming to steal your joy, take away your confidence, mess up your relationships, tempt you to doubt God's Word, and create chaos and havoc.

There's no condemnation in the fact that mind monsters are lurking in your life— everyone has them. You have a choice: Will you allow them to stay, affecting who you are and God's plan for your life, or will you conquer them?

Chapter 2

Faith Is the Exterminator

What do you think of when you read the word "faith"? You may think of all the misconceptions you've heard about it, including the assumption that people of faith are sadly mistaken, naïve, and uneducated.

But the fact is: <u>knowledge, understanding, and wisdom are compatible with a life of faith.</u>

People who possess a strong presence of faith automatically have fewer problems with mind monsters than those who don't. They are more likely to succeed in life due to less outside interference from the negative invaders of the mind.

We see great examples of this in our Bible heroes such as Moses, who attended the "Harvard" of his day; Solomon, who led major agricultural studies; and, the apostle Paul, who was a scholar and successful church leader.

Medical research confirms that those who attend church and behave consistent with their faith are *less likely* to abuse alcohol or drugs and receive treatment for stress or depression.

They are *more likely* to experience stable relationships, satisfaction in marriage and sex, and live healthier, more fulfilling lives.

When your faith becomes *big,* mind monsters become *small.* It's impossible to continue to live a life controlled by negativity when you have a growing presence of faith!

This realization anchors you in the understanding that faith is the exterminator of mind monsters!

An acronym for faith that has helped me increase its presence and power in my life is:

F — focus on the positive
A — affirm yourself
I — imagine God doing something good in your situation
T — trust God in all things
H — hope for the best

Focus on the positive. One of my pastor friends, Leon Fontaine, tells that before he went into the ministry, he was in training for the Olympics as a javelin thrower.

Day after day, he kept hearing what he was doing wrong. The more he focused on what was wrong, the worse his performance became.

Then a coach gave him a video of the world's best javelin thrower. Leon studied

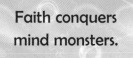

Faith conquers mind monsters.

the champion's form. Over and over, he

watched the way he released the javelin. When he changed his focus, immediately Leon's performance improved!

Similarly, on any given day, we all possess good and bad in our lives. As you're reading this book, you're bearing your share of troubles and enjoying your share of blessings in life. Your faith will grow when you focus on the positive!

Every day, you must decide what you're going to focus on. God won't decide for you—*you* must decide what your focus will be.

Ask yourself this question: *"Has my life improved when I've focused on all the negative things around me?"*

Positive minds produce positive lives; negative minds produce negative lives. Positive minds are always full of faith; negative minds are always full of mind monsters.

Affirm yourself. What do you say to yourself all day long? Don't underestimate the effect your internal dialogue has on your faith.

Are you allowing monsters of self-doubt to lead you down paths of insecurity and low self-worth? Instead, why not identify with the "you" that is in the metamorphosis of God's plan—the "you" that God is creating, rather than the "you" of your past or the "you" of your present!

Right now, maybe you're a caterpillar, but thank God you're on your way to becoming a butterfly. You can think of the "you" that's struggling to break out, the weak, little, no-winged caterpillar; or, you can focus on the "you" that is free, with strong enough wings that you're flying around, functioning the way God created you to be.

If you've ever experienced the joy of building a house, you know how much fun it is to drive out to the property when it's just a pile of dirt and the foundation's being poured. You invite your friends, and they all come along just to be nice.

> Focus on the "you" that is functioning the way God created you to be.

With blueprints in hand, you tell them, "The kitchen's going to be here, and the bedroom is going to be there. It's going to be this color. And the garage isn't going to be a one-car garage, but a three-car garage."

And your friends say, "That's beautiful, that's awesome. Now can we go and get something to eat?" But see, when it's under construction, you're excited about what will be, not what is.

Your enemy the mind monster wants you to focus on what you see right now: all of your failures and shortcomings, the "you" that doesn't measure up. That's what he wants you to think of in terms of "you." But God is saying, "No, there's a champion inside of you!"

It's good to recognize your weakness; to acknowledge you've messed up and repent of it. *Repentance* literally means "turning from your old ways." You completely turn away and face out toward the new "you."

So affirm yourself. Say "I have the mind of Christ" (see 1 Cor. 2:16) instead of chastising yourself for making another mistake. Say *"I can do all things through Christ who strengthens me"* (Phil. 4:13 NKJV) when you feel like you don't measure up. Don't give up! Affirm yourself!

Imagine God doing something good in your situation. I thank God for the power of imagination! He gave it to you to use for your good.

Therefore, when you pray, imagine your problem disappearing. When you pray, imagine your prayer being answered. Imagine your prodigal son or daughter, brother or sister, mom or dad coming to Christ and recommitting their life to Him. Imagine a job headed your way that you've been praying and believing God for. Imagine God at work doing something good for you!

In August of 2003, my wife, daughter, and I had an accident in Bermuda. Lying in a hospital room with a broken pelvis, I remember battling the thoughts in my mind: "Why did this happen to me? Here of all places! What a substandard hospital!"

Eight days passed before the staff cleaned out the deep cuts and wounds in my leg. I was wrestling with questions of, "Why, God? I'm your son. I'm a man of God. How could this happen to me here?"

The song "My Hope Is In The Name Of The Lord," inspired new hope and expectation within me. While listening repeatedly to it, I began to imagine: "I'm going to leave this place. I'm going to be well. I'm going to be healthy. Some great things are going to happen to people I meet here, through this situation I'm in."

I thank the Lord that great things did happen while I was there. I thank God for healing me. I'm whole and I'm well, getting better and stronger every day.

Someone asked me, "Pastor, if you could go back in time and avoid that accident in your life, would you?" Honestly from my heart, I can't say I wish this event never occurred, because of all the good things that have happened as a result.

But I really believe that all the good things were stimulated to happen because in my mind's eye, I saw God at work. I imagined how God was at work in that specific situation in my life right then. I still imagine Him at work in my life now.

Do you realize that right at this moment, God is working invisibly in your life to bring good things to you? *God's at work!* Imagine Him at work!

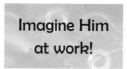
Imagine Him at work!

Trust God in all things. Think of God as always being with you. He's present even when you don't see him.

Living in Seattle, I've often experienced boarding a jet on a cloudy day, taking off, and then breaking through the clouds to see the sun shining in all its brightness! It's amazing how something that big and powerful can be hidden by clouds.

In the same way, when clouds enter some people's lives, they begin to doubt God's presence and goodwill toward them. That lack of confidence in God causes a disturbance deep within. Isaiah 26:3 says, *"You will keep in perfect peace him whose mind is steadfast, because he trusts in you."*

Hope for the best. Hope is what leads you to faith; you can't have faith without it. *"Faith is being sure of what we hope for and certain of what we do not see"* (Heb. 11:1 NKJV).

The best way to live your life is from a faith-initiated view of tomorrow. For example, imagine if I were to tell you that I want to bless you, so I have planned to send you on a very lucrative treasure hunt.

> The best way to live your life is from a faith-initiated view of tomorrow.

Tomorrow between 6:00 a.m. and 6:00 p.m., I have arranged for one thousand dollars to be placed in ten different locations waiting for you! I would give you the addresses, but you must make sure that you pick the money up between 6:00 a.m. and 6:00 p.m.

With hope and expectation in your heart, you would begin immediately to arrange your schedule so that you would have gained ten thousand dollars by the end of the day (of course dropping off your tithe before going home!):

- ✓ You would call work and request the day off
- ✓ You would set your alarm clock early enough to reach the first pickup point at 6:00 a.m.
- ✓ You might have to find transportation
- ✓ You might have to hire someone to take care of your children

But you would gladly do all of this, knowing you would be ten thousand dollars richer at the end of the day!

What if you lived your life this way, expecting great things from a God who wants to bless you and has treasures planned for you? All of your plans, actions, efforts, and attention would be focused on Him, expecting what God has promised to provide. Hope is the expectation of good things. So why not hope for the best?

I was never what I would call unhappy, but I had a "bend" in me that would be melancholy, too melancholy. When I was a young man, a pastor friend told me to get up in the morning, look in the mirror and say to myself, "I am happy, I am healthy, and I'm a Christian."

I remember how uncomfortable I was the first few days I did it. The mind monster kept answering me, "No you aren't, no you aren't, *no you aren't!*" But I kept confessing my faith, and I remember the result. When I visited my sister I hadn't seen in a long time, she said, "Kevin, I've noticed how much happier you seem to be. Your face looks happy."

Confessing, "I am happy, I am healthy, and I'm a Christian" caused my faith to grow which overpowered the melancholy invader of my mind.

To overcome mind monsters, build your faith until the force of faith inside you is stronger than the pressure of the negative invaders against you.

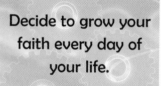

Decide to grow your faith every day of your life.

Two lions wage war inside you— faith and fear. Feed the lion of faith so it will grow. Starve the lion of fear so it will weaken and die. Decide to grow your faith every day of your life. When it grows, the less problem you'll have overcoming mind monsters in your everyday life.

Purposely grow your faith and use it to defeat mind monsters. Focus on the positive, affirm yourself, imagine God doing something good in your life, trust God in everything, and hope for the best!

Recognizing Mind Monsters

Recently, I participated in a golf tournament. Each foursome was given a yellow ball. If they were able to present their yellow ball at the end of eighteen holes, they qualified for a prize.

One member of a team would play the yellow ball on each hole, from the moment he teed off until he putted the ball into the cup. Then, he would pass the ball to another teammate, who would play the ball on the next hole, and so on.

My team's goal was to make sure we still had that yellow ball at the end of eighteen holes!

Every time it was someone's turn to play the ball, the other three guys would warn, "Don't mess up! Make sure it doesn't go in the pond. Make sure it doesn't go in the woods. Hit the ball straight. Play it safe. Keep the yellow ball!" We would cheer for each another, challenging the guardian of the yellow ball!

I had a special event to attend that night, so I had to leave after nine holes. Rushing, I threw my golf clubs in the car and was heading out on the highway when my cell phone rang. I heard my teammates on the other end of the phone screaming, "You've got the yellow ball!" I felt my pocket and sure enough, I had it! I hadn't even known I had it!

That's the way it is with mind monsters. Most people who have them don't recognize they have them. Before you can overcome a mind monster, you must recognize its presence in your life.

Do you know it's easier to recognize someone else's mind monsters than your own? You may be reading this book and thinking, "I hope my husband (wife) will read this. He really needs it! Oh, I wish my boss would get a copy—he could definitely use this."

Have you ever heard someone say, "I'm not negative, I'm a realist," and the people who hear them

> It's easier to recognize someone else's mind monsters than your own.

are shocked! Or someone says, "I'm not worried, I'm just concerned." We place our own spin on our mind-set, alleviating the reality of what it really is.

The interesting thing about mind monsters is that they sound like your own inner voice of reason. It's easy to not recognize a mind monster when it walks through the doorway of your mind because it sounds so much like you. Its entrance is subtle.

So how do you recognize mind monsters in your life? There are three easy ways. Pay attention to your:

- Internal dialogue
- Moods
- Conversation

Ask yourself, "What effect is my internal dialogue having on me? How does the dialogue in my head cause me to feel and behave?"

Consider the story of Jason, a man who was healthy and had many friends, but who was a notorious worrier. One summer day, the train crew he worked with was informed they could quit an hour early. As the crew prepared to go home, Jason was accidentally locked in a refrigerated boxcar.

Realizing what happened, he shouted and banged on the door, but no one noticed. Jason began to worry, thinking to himself, "If I don't get out of here, I'll freeze."

With a rusty screw he found lying on the floor, Jason etched these words on the boxcar wall: "It's so cold. My body is getting numb. These may be my last words."

The next morning, the crew slid the heavy doors of the boxcar open and found Jason lying unconscious on the floor. They quickly rushed him to the hospital, where the medical personnel reported that Jason's body had the physical signs of hypothermia.

However, when the crew returned to the work site, they discovered that the boxcar's refrigeration unit was inoperative, and the temperature inside was a moderate fifty-five degrees! Jason's fear and worry had changed his physiology.

If Jason's story seems extreme to you, what does it take to make *your* heart race in the middle of the night? Merely *thinking* you hear a noise?

If you get lost in the woods in a don't-feed-the-bears territory and *think* you hear the brush moving and stirring around you, a cold sweat will top your brow, your heart will beat wildly, and your knees will knock together! And to think, your internal dialogue is driving it all!

When the voice in your head is talking, are you becoming stronger or weaker? More confident or more timid?

When Paul the apostle wrote to the young preacher, Timothy, he was appealing to him to recognize his inner dialogue. He said, "God didn't give you that spirit of timidity. You need to recognize that's not coming from God" (see 2 Tim. 1:7).

Another time, when writing to a church in Corinth, he said, "Look, God hasn't given us a spirit of confusion. God's not the author of confusion" (see 1 Cor. 14:33). If you're confused, angry, or discouraged, you have mind monsters. If you're judgmental, untrusting, worried about people liking you, or if you're always assuming the worst, then guess what? You have mind monsters!

Do you recognize and oppose them? Or do you deny that you have them?

I want you to look with me at two examples in Scripture showing how internal dialogue affected a person's life. A woman who was hemorrhaging for twelve years came to Jesus for healing. Fortunately, her internal dialogue was positive. The Bible records that she told herself, *"If I only touch his cloak, I will be healed"* (Matt. 9:21).

She was able to reach Him, and when she touched His garment, twelve years of suffering ended just like that! A lot of people were touching Jesus that day, but when *she* touched Him, her healing was activated because of what she said within herself.

But a servant in Matthew 25:14-30 had a negative internal dialogue. His master entrusted his talents (unit of money) to three servants; the first servant received five, the second received two, and the third received one.

When the master required an accounting of the money, he was pleased to find that the servants to whom he had given five and ten talents had doubled his money. He promptly rewarded them both.

The master was displeased to discover that the third servant had buried his one talent in the ground. The servant explained, *"I was afraid and went out and hid your talent in the ground"* (v. 25). Instead of rewarding him as he had the others, the master wasted no time in punishing him.

This servant's internal dialogue took over the driver's seat of his life, creating a fear inside him that caused him to bury the one talent that could have meant prosperity, increase, **The woman, who told herself she would be healed, received what she hoped for.** and growth in his life. But the woman, who told herself she would be healed, received what she hoped for.

If you want to recognize mind monsters, take a good look at how your internal dialogue is affecting you.

The second way to recognize mind monsters in your life is to pay attention to your moods. Today, are you upbeat or down in the dumps? Your feelings spring from your thoughts, and thoughts originate in the mind.

How healthy is your mind? To know, take a good look at your mood! The Bible refers to your mood as the "spirit" of your mind. Ephesians 4:23 AMP tells you to *"be constantly renewed in the spirit of your mind [having a fresh mental and spiritual attitude.]"*

As you read this book, you may be thinking about how much you hate mind monsters and want them out of your life. You're thinking about faith, and how to grow it.

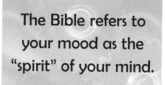

The Bible refers to your mood as the "spirit" of your mind.

But even though you're focusing on this, probably sometime today, something will happen that tempts you to feel upset. You may find yourself in a traffic jam, where you can feel annoyed, or you can decide to put on a Christian CD so that the music or preaching can renew your mind.

If you want to live a victorious Christian life, you have to constantly renew the mood of your mind.

Why do you turn the music on? Why do you speak the Word of God into your life? Why do you read the Word? Why do you talk yourself happy? You do these things to constantly renew the mood of your mind!

The third way to recognize mind monsters in your life is to pay attention to your conversation. Let's take a look at a couple named Brenda and Tony. Brenda is constantly nagging Tony about what's he doing wrong and what she doesn't like about him.

She says things like, "Why do you wear ties? And silver ones at that? And that hair on your face! What a dork you are! You're useless."

You may be thinking, "Wow! I know what needs to happen. Brenda needs Jesus.

After she's born again, this issue will go away." That's how a lot of Christians think.

Guess what? Brenda *is* saved. Brenda already has Jesus in her life and she's on her way to heaven!

Brenda has one problem. She has a mind monster. The mind monster causes her to always focus on the negative. She subconsciously thinks she's called to be the faultfinder in her world. It may be the faults in her kids, her husband, or her job, but she spotlights them as if she'll win a reward!

Your conversation gives away the presence of a mind monster.

How can she recognize it? By paying attention to her faultfinding, critical conversation.

Recognizing mind monsters is the first step to eliminating them, while denying their presence allows them to stay. Over the next three days, pay attention to your internal dialogue, moods, and conversation. What's there?

Chances are you will recognize negativity you had somehow overlooked. At that point, you're ready to move on to the next step and get busy rejecting their influence in your life.

Chapter 4

Rejecting
Mind Monsters

Do you realize your mind's power to influence and, in some cases, create your reality? Your life will be defined by the thoughts you accept or reject.

One day, I listened as a neighbor described how he was raising his nine-year-old daughter.

He said, "We're not attending one church. We're taking her to all the different religions to expose her to a broad spectrum. Then, if she doesn't want to go to church, that

> Your life will be defined by the thoughts you accept or reject.

will be fine. She won't have to go. We're just going to give her a broad, open-minded perspective of everything."

I replied, "So what happens if she doesn't want to go to school tomorrow?"

He exclaimed, "Oh, no! She must go to school because she has to get an education."

So I countered, *"There's no absolute?* You're not going to be open minded about that?"

He said, "No, because education really affects where you go in life."

We live in a time when people are so open minded they have no "true north" in their life. They hear a thought and open their mind to it. Then they hear another idea and open their mind to that as well.

They are so open minded, they end up entertaining every thought that shows up. They have "the inquiring mind." They think, "I want to go investigate that, I want to experience that kind of movie, I want to read that book, I want to listen to that idea, I want to consider that concept."

Eventually, they lack discretion and judgment. They adhere to *no* absolutes—they argue with the compass.

The true north principles in the universe were established by God, not by society. You will find them in His Word, where Psalm 1:1-3, 6 AMP says, *"Blessed*

> The true north principles in the universe were established by God.

(happy, fortunate, prosperous, and enviable) is the man . . . [whose] delight and desire are in the . . . (teachings of God), [on which] he habitually meditates (ponders, and studies) by day and by night . . . everything he does shall prosper . . . but the way of the ungodly [those living outside God's will] shall perish."

The more you live in harmony with God's principles, the better your life will be. You will experience greater joy, greater peace, and greater success.

The more you ignore these true north principles, the greater the challenges you will encounter, the more lost and abandoned you will feel, and the more insecure and unsure of yourself you will become.

Second Corinthians 10:5 teaches that we must recognize and destroy thoughts that are inconsistent with God's thoughts: *"We demolish arguments and every pretension that sets itself up against the knowledge of God, and we take captive every thought to make it obedient to Christ."*

Jesus demonstrated this when Peter expressed his disapproval of Jesus' impending suffering and death: ". . . *he rebuked Peter. 'Get behind me, Satan! . . . You do not have in mind the things of God, but [rather] the things of men'* " (Mark 8:33). He was rejecting the thought Peter spoke that originated in hell.

Therefore, I'm going to give you two principles to help you *accept* true north thoughts and *reject* mind monster thoughts in your life:

1. Commit to a P4-8 standard for your thoughts.
2. Activate a border patrol to guard your mind.

What is a P4-8 standard for your thoughts? P4-8 stands for Philippians 4:8 which says, *"Finally brothers, whatever is true, whatever is noble, whatever is right, whatever is pure, whatever is lovely, whatever is admirable—if anything is excellent or praiseworthy—think about such things."*

If a thought is true, but not noble, don't think about it. If it's not pure, admirable, or lovely, don't dwell on it. When you hear someone say, "Life is hard; it's so tough!" you don't have to accept it—you can reject that thought. This Scripture is saying: Don't give mental energy to a thought unless it passes the P4-8 standard.

If you own a champion racehorse you think has a chance to win the Kentucky Derby, you're not going to feed that racehorse ketchup and peanut butter. You're going to look for the highest quality of oats you can find. You're going to want to know exactly what's going into the horse's body to achieve the greatest results; you understand that feeding the horse the right food directly relates to the horse's performance.

Don't give mental energy to a thought unless it passes the P4-8 standard.

Your mind is more valuable than a racehorse! If you want to position yourself for success, you must accept the fact that what you allow into your mind will affect the outcome of your life.

If you use a computer, you're familiar with the "delete" button. When you scan through your daily e-mails, you identify what you're interested in by looking at the subject lines. When you see something you choose not to take time with, you hit the delete button. Delete, delete, delete! *You* are the thinker of your own thoughts! It's easy to blame others, such as your parents, the media, or Hollywood influencers. In reality, you choose what you're going to allow in.

I remember an occasion years ago when a wife came to me about a problem with her husband. She was ready to get rid of him, turn him in. He didn't measure up.

I said to her, "Would you do me a favor? Would you just simply go home today and begin to try to find ten good things about your husband this week? If you could find ten good things about him and focus on them, I believe your situation will begin to turn around."

I'm happy to say that now, ten or more years later, I still see this couple in church; they are together and doing extremely well. It seems like I never get a birthday note or a Christmas card from this grateful wife without a thank you for my challenge to focus on the positive.

After you decide to think only the thoughts that pass the P4-8 standard, set up a border patrol for your mind. This is the action you take to enforce the P4-8 standard, the policing of thoughts that try to steal your success in life.

North of Seattle, Washington, there's a patrol that scrutinizes every person before they cross the border between Canada and the United States. Once when my wife, Sheila, and

I were traveling, they pulled us out of line and into their building. They thoroughly checked us out.

After it was all over, I enjoyed teasing my wife, telling her that *she* was the one who looked suspicious! I told her I wasn't going to bring her with me the next time! We had a lot of fun with it.

All through the examination, we expressed our thanks to the border patrol because we understood they were there to reject travelers who planned to hurt our nation. We understood the value of the scrutiny; we appreciated the fact they were there to protect us.

An unguarded mind is an unprotected mind. Patrol your mind by rejecting every thought that doesn't meet the P4-8 standard. Stop it from crossing over into your mind, where it can ruin your relationships and defeat your dreams. Proverbs 4:23 reads,

"Above all else, guard your heart, for it is the wellspring of life." Here, the word "heart" is interchangeable with the words "mind" and "soul," so the writer is stressing that whatever you do, above all else, set up a border patrol to guard your mind!

A simple rubber band can help you understand how to patrol your mind. Find a rubber band and encircle one thumb with it. Pull way back on it with the index finger of your other hand, saying, "I reject this negative thought (name it)!" Let go of it! Pull it back again and say, "I delete you!" Let it snap! After you apply this exercise enough times, even the mention of a negative thought will become a sore spot in your life!

Above all else, set up a border patrol to guard your mind!

Recently I saw a movie called "Raising Helen." The main character is a single woman who becomes the custodian of her sister's children after their parents die in an automobile accident. She enrolls the children in a Christian school, where she meets the pastor who oversees it. They're both single, and immediately there's a chemistry between them.

I love the way the movie portrays the pastor. Usually, I don't like the way Hollywood depicts Christians or pastors because they appear to be freaks—abnormal and weird. I don't enjoy the spin they place on that role. But in this movie, the pastor's a contemporary, normal guy who plays ice hockey and hangs out with his friends. He loves God; he's given his life to Him.

He's attracted to the leading lady in the movie, and contemplates how to date her. She won't have anything to do with dating him—she has the religious mind-set that he's a priest who can't get married.

When he says, "Let's go have dinner," she says, "No, I don't want to make you lose your religion." All he wants is to have dinner and pursue a social relationship. He replies, "I may be in the ministry, but I'm not weird. I'm a man. In my religion, I can get married and have children."

As I watched the movie, I liked this guy more and more. I was privately cheering him on, because I know many ministers like him. They're great people who aren't stuck back in time. They're living the Christian life right now, relating to a modern and contemporary world. They're rational, intellectual people.

In one scene, the minister and the lady are standing in a doorway. He's talking to her, still trying to convince her to go to dinner with him. She's still nervous about it, and putting him off. Finally, he takes a step backward and proclaims, "Well, I just want to tell you that I'm a sexy man of God and I know it!"

This leading man did not internalize someone else's inaccurate image of him! He was saying, "I reject that. You might try to put me in a box, but I know who I am. I may wear this collar, but don't count me out, babe! I'm a man you'd love to spend the rest of your life with!"

You see, you don't have to accept every thought that people hold about you or the image they try to project on you. As a believer in your workplace, I hope you don't allow people to intimidate you. You're the one that's got it going on! If you don't fit into your coworkers' ideas of who you should be because you love God and believe in morals, reject their thoughts!

Over the years, Sheila and I have had to fight to have the kind of church we have now. On a regular basis, we reject and resist people's ideas that try to put us in a religious box. Especially when the church was younger and smaller, people's impressions of church (stained-glass windows and boring organ music) collided with ours. We expect church to be relevant and helpful.

If you stop and ask most people why they don't go to church, they respond with, "Hello! It's boring and it doesn't help me at all." Listen, I believe most people aren't rejecting the good news of the Gospel— they're rejecting the *package* it's in.

God has called my wife and me to pastor a church that relates to this generation. Jesus related to His generation. He talked to them in their language of agricultural and shepherding terms. We talk to our generation in a language they understand.

When people look down on us because of this, we don't allow them to make us feel shallow and that our faith isn't authentic. We know our faith is authentic! We know we love God with all of our hearts and we know we're committed to His kingdom.

I watched the television coverage of the 2004 Tour de France when Lance Armstrong was close to winning a stage of the race, yet wanted one of his teammates to have the opportunity to win it instead. Lance was encouraging him by talking and waving him on. They were just a few kilometers away from the finish line. Lance was slowing down and blocking another racer, while saying to his U.S.A. teammate, "Go! Win a stage."

All of a sudden, a racer from another country sped by them and took the lead. Although he was far behind, I could see that "tiger look" appear in Lance's eyes as he started aiming and pedaling. Like a real champion, I could tell he was thinking, *"That's* not going to happen today!"

He stood on his bike and cranked away. He crossed the finish line, one bicycle wheel ahead of his opponent, hands held high in the air! Afterwards during an interview, he said, "I just wanted the other guy, my friend on my team, to be able to win a stage."

When people say, "Everyone's out for themselves—everyone!" you can either accept or reject that thinking. You can buy into the idea that everyone's out for themselves, or you can notice people like Lance who go out of their way to do something generous and kind. You will find them when you look for them.

The Bible emphasizes that your mind is a battlefield where you win or lose in life. Your life will turn out very differently, depending on which thoughts you accept and reject.

Chapter 5

Replacing Mind Monsters

In Jesus' most famous message, the Sermon on the Mount, all six points began like this: "You have heard, *but I say* to you" (see Matt. 5). He was saying to the listener and to all of us today that He wants to replace the thinking we have acquired from others with a higher way of thinking. Jesus was teaching the principle of replacing old thoughts with new and better ones.

You see, mind monsters often invade your mind in the form of ideas, concepts, and philosophies transferred to you from others. God is saying to you today that He wants to replace your old, negative, oppressive thought life you picked up along life's way—perhaps in the home you grew up in, or in school from a teacher you admired, at college or work, or from hanging out with friends—with a new, higher, better way of thinking.

Have you ever noticed that when you tell yourself to stop thinking about something, it becomes the thing you think of most? In early American history, traveling magicians would sell villagers a special powder they claimed would turn water into gold, provided that when the villagers mixed it, they would never think of red monkeys.

Of course, no one ever got the gold because *when you tell yourself to not think about red monkeys, that's exactly what you think of!*

Likewise, if you tell yourself to not think about something . . . guess what you think about? . . . And worry about? . . . You must move on! How?

- Realize that God will help you take control of your mind—you're not on your own!
- Fill your mind with P4-8 thoughts.
- Look for wisdom as if there's a reward!

First of all, know that God is *ready* to help you take control of your mind. God *wants* to help free you from thoughts of worry, fear, lust, and anxiety. He gave you the Bible which instructs how He thinks— His ideas, perspectives, and thoughts—and how you can think like He does.

The second thing to know about replacing a mind monster is to *fill* your mind every day with thoughts that meet the P4-8 standard. Ask yourself: Am I full of true, noble, right, pure, lovely, admirable, excellent, and praiseworthy thoughts? Replace a mind monster by filling your mind every day with thoughts that meet the P4-8 standard.

W. Clement Stone said, "Keep your mind off the things that you don't want, by keeping it on the things you do want." The most effective remedy for bad thinking is good thinking.

> Replace a mind monster by filling your mind every day with thoughts that meet the P4-8 standard.

So ask yourself this question: How often do I think good, faith-based thoughts—focusing on the positive, affirming myself, imagining God doing something good on my behalf, trusting God in every situation, and hoping for the best?

Now if the answer is that it's often—very, very often—then the correlating truth is that there's very little opportunity for negative thoughts to invade your mind. You see, if you're thinking faith thoughts often enough, then a negative invader will be like a car pulling into a shopping mall on Christmas Eve looking for a parking space — it will wander around trying to find a place to park, but all the spaces will be full!

However, if you realize you don't think faith-based thoughts very often, you probably realize you're leaving a lot of space up there that something is going to fill! Regardless if your mind is a three-decker parking lot or a one-level parking lot, if you fill your mind every day with thoughts that meet the P4-8 standard, then there will be no space for worry, evil imaginations, fear, discouragement, insecurity, and inferiority.

Do you often ponder, "I wonder if they like me or not? What do they think of me? I bet they think I'm stupid"? Don't allow space for that! Replace those thoughts with, "What great people I know! I'm sure they're thinking kind thoughts about me."

After you've rejected mind monsters, their parking spots are empty. They'll find their way back in, settling right back into your mind, unless you fill their empty spots by thinking differently (*replacing* the mind monster thoughts).

Repetition is what helps you deposit good thoughts into your memory bank.

Stock up on some tools that help you fill your mind with good things, such as a Bible you will actually read and understand and Christian music CDs.

Another great idea is to memorize a quote a month. Choose a verse and memorize it. Say it over and over again. Repetition is what helps you deposit it into your memory bank. After a year, you'll have twelve of them stored up. After two years, you'll have twenty-four. A few years of memorizing the

Word will fill the spaces of your conscious and subconscious mind.

My wife fills our house with music. As she moves from one area to another in our home, she listens to different radio or cable TV stations. It never occurs to her that I walk through the house and get totally confused! I'll find myself in the middle of an upbeat, fast song, then walk to the other end of the house and hear something slow and therapeutic. But she's filling up every square inch of the house with something good and positive!

Do the same thing with your mind. Fill your mind with good things!

Last, look for wisdom as if there's a reward! There is! Proverbs 9:12 says, *"If you are wise, your wisdom will reward you."*

It's just as easy to be wise as it is to be foolish, in the sense that it's all in a choice you make. The price to obtain wisdom may be higher, but the decision to be wise is easier to make based on what wisdom will do for your performance in life.

When you pull your car into a filling station, you select the octane level of the gas you're going to put into the engine. You can choose a low grade or a high grade. A high-performance automobile uses high-grade fuel because it will perform better. You will perform better in life if you choose to be wise.

Wisdom is available if you seek it. God doesn't hide wisdom and say, "Too bad! I hope you can find it!" If you've never read Proverbs 1-3, I recommend you do. It tells you that wisdom is findable; it's not hiding.

Wisdom is not education. That's why someone can earn a degree, author a book on marriage but then get divorced; while a simple couple with only an eighth grade education can have a fantastic life together.

Wisdom was God's first creation. The Bible says that wisdom was the craftsman of the universe, meaning that the entire universe was formed by wisdom (see Jer. 10:12)! So, the more you agree with wisdom, the more you act in wisdom, the better your life will be—less heartache, less crisis, less turmoil.

> The more you act in wisdom, the better your life will be.

The Bible says what wisdom provides you is greater than silver (see Prov. 3:13-14). If you take time to hear her voice, she will speak to you.

Sometimes you hit a place in life where something's not right or wrong—it's wise or unwise. Take the example of two young people graduating from high school, and one asks himself, "What college do I want to go to?" Another says, "I don't want to go to college."

Well, I can't say everyone must go to college. I can't say it's wrong to not want to pursue a secondary education. However, I will say that when you hit a crossroad in life, don't follow your natural impulses and instincts. Don't make a decision based on what your natural flesh craves, because it will probably crave no more school, no more books, and no more education.

But wisdom may say to you, "God has an awesome plan for your life and your future, and I would advise you to go and get your education. Position yourself where God's will can be fulfilled in your life, and the only way you can do that is more school, more books, and more education."

Some single adults think, "I can't wait to get married." The natural instincts are "I'm lonely. I want to be wanted." The natural impulses are "I want to be loved. I don't want to live the rest of my life without a partner." But wisdom provides an elevated thought life. Wisdom says there's something worse than being single, and that is being married to the wrong person.

Welcome wisdom. Want wisdom. The world has its own way of thinking; the world has its own ideas. As you walk through life, you have to be careful not to copy the decision-making instincts of society.

You have to say, "Wait just a minute. I recognize a mind monster getting into my psyche, leading me down a road of destruction, and I can't afford to think that way. I have to elevate my mind to a higher way of thinking. I don't have to fear that no one's going to want me. I don't have to fear that I'm going to live the rest of my life alone. I can focus on the positive and affirm myself. I can imagine God doing something good and I can trust God even now while I'm single. I will hope for the best in my life and future."

When negative information tempts your mind, declare, "I reject you. You can be replaced, because you're not produced from faith. You're from fear and doubt. Many have walked down your pathway and have ended in major crises in life. I'm going to choose the path of wisdom. The price might be a little higher, but I'm going to go for the high-octane stuff, because I want a better life."

Jesus loved to talk about wisdom. He said, "A foolish man builds a house on the sand and the storms of life come and the house collapses. But a wise man builds his house on a solid foundation and the wind blows and the rain comes and the storm comes and the house stands firm" (see Matt. 7: 24-27). Jesus wasn't talking about a physical house; He was talking about the life you build.

He's encouraging you to build your life on wise thoughts. Watch for wisdom; fill your day with it. Instead of being drawn toward negative invaders of the mind, don't allow space for them. Listen for someone to say something wise. Write it down, memorize it. Say it over and over, adding, "Oh, that's good. I'm going to keep that close to my heart. I'm going to put that in my mind. I'm going to build up an inventory

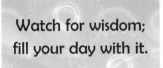

Watch for wisdom; fill your day with it.

of wisdom inside me so wisdom flows out of my life like a river. When I have a decision to make, I'm going to make a wise choice, not a foolish one. I will be full of wisdom."

I love the story that a friend of mine named Joseph Garlington tells. He said a university professor was computing grades at the end of a semester. A female student approached him the night before the grades were to be released. Walking into his office wearing a tight white top, she perched seductively on his desk, and whispered, "What can I do to get a good grade?" The professor, a man of God, threw her out of his office and ran home!

As soon as he stepped inside the door, he called out for his wife: "Come here. Go to the bedroom, put on a white T-shirt, and walk down these steps. I have a thought I've got to get out, and I want to replace it with a better one. Come to me, honey!"

When some men try to overcome lust, they stay focused on the very image they want to get out of their mind. Even though they want to get that woman out of their mind, they approach it in a way that keeps her in their mind, saying, "I won't think about that woman. I'm not going to think about her. I rebuke that thought. I rebuke that woman!"

And they just stay there, stuck on the thought they're trying to reject! What are they doing all week? They're thinking about the woman!

But the professor in this story understood the secret of replacing a mind monster with a positive thought.

First, recognize a mind monster, then reject it, and afterward, replace it with a thought of faith and confidence. Finally, I'll show you how to retrain your mind to become the person you aspire to be.

Retraining Your Mind

Computers seem to be everywhere today—in homes, offices, and even in cars. How a computer works is similar to how your mind works.

My automobile has a computer that tells me when I have a flat tire. After Sunday service during one of our church conferences, my wife and I took some of our guest pastors out to lunch. On our way to the restaurant, my dashboard illuminated two words: Flat tire!

Immediately, I felt anxious. Glancing over at Sheila, I exclaimed, "Great! What a time for a flat tire! Can you believe it? We have a flat tire!"

I apologized to the people in the backseat. "I'm sorry. We have a flat tire." My mind was reeling: "Why do I have a flat tire now? Why did it happen on a Sunday when I'm wearing a suit? Why couldn't this happen another time?" Suddenly, another thought occurred to me: "Maybe I can make it to the restaurant and call a tow truck." We made it! I hurried out of the car to examine the tires. They all looked good—everything was fine! We shrugged, and walked inside the restaurant.

Halfway through our meal, one of the men in our group left to check the tires. When he reappeared, he said the tires looked great. He commented that it looked like there was no problem at all.

When we finished our meal, we started the car to head home. Immediately, the dashboard blazed: Flat tire, flat tire, flat tire!

Being the handyman I am, when I arrived home, I pulled out my tire pressure gauge. Yes, being the handyman I am, I checked the pressure in all of the tires. The pressure was fine! So I walked inside the house, and waited to see what would happen in the morning.

On Monday morning, I examined the tires again. They all looked fine. As I headed for the office, the infamous red light announced: Flat tire, flat tire, flat tire! At that moment, I recognized what was going on! I said to myself, "My car has a mind monster and I know exactly what to do!"

In a gesture of fun, I announced, "I *recognize* you! I *reject* you! My tire's not flat. You're a liar!" I continued, "I *replace* you— I'm going to override you right now. I'm going to act like you don't exist. I'm going to keep driving to the office. I'm going to keep riding in this car. Nothing is wrong."

I made it to the office and I made it back home. On Tuesday, the car made it everywhere I needed to go. All week long, the car made it everywhere I had to go, and all week long that red dashboard light lied to me!

Every time I heard new passengers gasp at the warning light, I applied the three R's: "I recognize you, I reject you, I replace you." I explained to my companions, "Don't worry about it, it's wrong. It's a mind monster. It doesn't know what it's talking about. Just agree with me that everything's fine."

On Friday, I took the car to the shop and explained to the mechanic, "The mind of my car isn't functioning right. Would you please reprogram it?" He did just that—he retrained the computer in my car and it hasn't lied to me since!

Retrain your mind. To get rid of a mind monster, recognize it, reject it, replace it, and then retrain your mind to think differently.

How do you retrain your mind? First, realize that your mind automatically thinks in habitual patterns. In other words, your mind is a creation of habit; the brain cells of your computer (mind) record each step of your decisions in order to be repeated. Do you notice that you dress the same way every morning? When you put on your pants, notice that you begin with the same foot every day.

Your mind automatically thinks in habitual patterns.

This is because your brain has recorded each dressing step as a "habit." It can be a scary thing to drive all the way home from work and realize you weren't consciously aware of the road or traffic. Pulling into your driveway, all of a sudden you realize, "Oh, I'm home!" You made every turn, stopped at every light, and didn't run anyone off the road. Your subconscious mind worked for you and brought you home that day.

That's the power of the human mind. But you have to realize God created it to work for your good, not to work against you. Show your mind what to do, and it automatically picks up on it. Unfortunately, many times this same great mind picks up a negative train of thought, and falls into a rut of habitual worry, doubt, fear, skepticism, or criticism. Your mind will remain this way until you consciously make an effort to reprogram it.

I remember going horseback riding as a child with my family, when my parents took us to one of those trail-riding stables. It didn't take long for me to realize it was *boring!* When I wanted the horse to run or veer off the beaten path a little, I would command, "Giddyap!" I would kick the horse or pull on the reins! But that horse would just stay right there, on the same old familiar trail. I caught on quickly that this horse was doing nothing except following the others in a line and going down the same trail as always.

Your mind works in much the same way. Just as it takes a determined effort, a strong will, and authority to make a trail horse turn off the beaten path, ("Horse, we're not going down this trail right now. I'm your master, and we're going over here"), it also takes authority to take your mind down a new trail.

In other words, it's one thing to recognize, reject, and replace mind monsters. But you must also retrain your mind by doing the process continually! Keep recognizing, keep rejecting, and keep replacing them!

You can't expect to have a different mind-set within twenty-four hours, or even forty-eight. Some psychologists say it takes a minimum of eleven days—others as much as twenty-one days—to create a new habit.

After my family moved to a new home, I left the office one day and drove all the way to our former house before I realized I didn't live there anymore! Your mind develops a mental rut and dictates your direction. Until you realize you have to interrupt the old pattern and consciously say, "I'm going to retrain you to think a new and better way," your mind will stay on that same, old, familiar trail of thought.

> Interrupt the old pattern and consciously say, "I'm going to retrain you to think a new and better way."

How much energy do you expend on mind monsters that jump into your life, taking you down trails where you don't want to go? Consider Doris's story. After work one day, she sat down with her husband and said, "I have to talk to you. Something's really bothering me." She continued, "I have cancer."

Shocked, he said, "What do you mean you have cancer? Did the doctor examine you?"

She said, "No, but my boss died of cancer and I remember the evolution of the disease. He had headaches, and I've had headaches for the last few days. He said his lips started turning numb, and this morning when I left the house on my way to work, my lips were turning numb."

At this point, her husband broke out in laughter. That didn't help her, so feeling frustrated, she burst, "Why are you laughing? This isn't funny. *This isn't funny—I have cancer!* Do you understand?"

By this time, he was in a ball of stitches, laughing up a storm. Finally, she demanded, "What's wrong!"

Composing himself, he explained, "Honey, before you left for work this morning, do you remember we kissed good-bye?"

"Yes," she replied.

He continued, "Well, I had just applied numbing medication to my lip for a fever blister!" (Doris needed a rubber band to snap for a while!)

If you're thinking, "But I do have cancer; my doctor has given me the report," I say to you all the more: You need God's help to fight the battle against mind monsters. He hasn't given you *"a spirit of fear, but of power and of love and of a sound mind"* (2 Tim. 1:7 NKJV)! Just as it takes time and effort to allow a mind monster to master your mind, it takes time and effort to master a new positive mental habit. Which way do you choose to live?

Have you ever thought much about your habits (observable tendencies and characteristics that form your behavior patterns)? And that when people watch you, they notice your habits and then describe you that way? How do you want to be described? *Who do you really want to be?*

Some people are described as funny. They are habitually funny, habitually finding humor in everything. When you're around them, you expect to laugh a lot. They're funny because their mind is programmed that way; they probably received a few laughs when they were young, they enjoyed bringing pleasure to people, and consequently, their mind picked up on that train of thought. Now, they're funny and we call them funny.

Then there are other people who find humor in nothing. People describe them as sad, gloomy, or negative. But about somebody else we might say, "They're the most upbeat, positive person you'll ever want to meet."

A young man commented to me, "I know my father is going to be angry with me." I thought to myself, "How does he know that? How can he predict that?" But then I quickly realized, "His conclusion has to be based on past experience." The father behaved in a predictable pattern of anger.

> Decide and declare what kind of person you want to be and direct your mind toward that goal.

Why do we describe people as funny, sad, or angry? Because they *are* that way—habitually and automatically!

Decide and declare what kind of person you want to be and direct your mind toward that goal. A science called "neuro-linguistic programming"—"neuro" meaning "brain" and "linguistic" meaning "language"—verifies Bible teachings that your mind and your words work together to create thinking patterns.

As strange as it may sound, most people don't think about what kind of person they want to become—they just become what they become. They accept the first thought they have and become whatever that thought causes them to become. They subconsciously conform to the thinking pattern of the world. Rather than deciding and declaring what kind of person they want to be, they allow their surroundings to shape and mold them.

You may reason, "You don't understand my life. You don't understand what's happened to me." Sometimes people justify their negative mind-set this way. They justify living in worry, intimidation, and fear. Have you justified staying on the same negative trail of thought, blaming the events and the circumstances of your life?

If you drive down an old logging trail or dirt road in the Great Northwest, often your tires will bump along the ruts in the road. Sometimes, vehicles get stuck in the deep ruts and have a hard time getting out.

Likewise, you can get stuck in the deep mental ruts that reach into and take over all your patterns of thinking. To get "unstuck," you have to be willing as a child of God to take Romans 12:2 as your own: *Do not conform any longer to the [thinking] pattern of this world, but be transformed by the renewing of your mind.* Here, the apostle Paul is clearly saying, "This is how you ought to think."

In other words, don't let the old trail dictate to you—carve out a new trail! Don't allow your mind to take you down the familiar easy road it has memorized through mental rut territory. Interrupt those negative thoughts: recognize, reject, and replace them until your negative habits disappear. Retrain your brain to new habits by deciding who you want to become, declaring it, and renewing your mind with the Word of God until you become the person you want to be.

Do you wonder if this really works? Consider how retraining the mind lowers the repeat offender rate of former prisoners in the United States. The world's largest prison population per capita resides in the U.S.; there are more people incarcerated there than in any other nation in the world (two million people in 2004). Unfortunately, there's not a lot of hope for them, even after they're released, because studies show they have over a 50 percent chance of returning again for a similar offense.

In response to this, in the last few years beginning with a prison in Florida, there are now faith-based prison programs. In fact, Florida has the first all faith-based prison.

Convicted people can decide not to go there; however, the prison has all they can handle because most people *want* to go there.

Why? They're experiencing great results! The reoffender rate has decreased significantly in these prisons. Because you can't argue with results, this program has overflowed into other states.

In these prisons, the lifestyle is geared toward faith. Prisoners attend worship services where they praise and worship God. They encourage each other. The employees are believers, so when prisoners find themselves at a crossroad in life, they pray about it together. They read the Scriptures daily and apply them by faith. They encourage each other with their faith. Prisoners are leaving this system with the hope they won't return because they have retrained their minds. They're thinking a new way! They found a way to get out of the old mental rut!

Why wait until you're facing divorce? Why wait until you encounter a huge financial crisis? Why wait until you do something in a fit of anger that lands you in a prison cell? Why not begin today to retrain your mind?

Benjamin Franklin, a great hero and leader in our nation, understood this principle. As a young man, he wrote down thirteen virtues he wanted to exemplify. He focused on one virtue each week, aiming at absorbing that virtue into his behavior. In thirteen weeks' time, he cycled through all the virtues on his piece of paper. He repeated this sequence four times each year.

I think it's exciting to read about this famous man who took the responsible step of literally gathering a piece of paper and a writing instrument, and then writing down virtues that proclaimed, "This is the kind of man I want to be." Benjamin Franklin understood that to become a better person, he must lead his mind down a new trail of habitual thought.

As a person who desires a new life, new future, and a new legacy, you can't afford certain habitual thoughts to remain in your mind. For the sake of your future, your children's, and your legacy, choose to change thoughts currently programmed into your mind that block your way to a better life.

Writing down who you want to be activates change!

Writing down who you want to be may seem a trivial exercise, but it activates change! I invite you right now to write down three words, maybe five if you're feeling ambitious, that describe the kind of person you want to be.

The person I want to be is:

1. _____ 4. _____
2. _____ 5. _____
3. _____

What kind of words did you write down? Happy, generous, serving? Encouraging, obedient, strong, influential, trustworthy? Generous, consistent, hospitable, positive? I bet you didn't write: negative, discouraging, worrier, unhappy, mad.

Do you know why? Because God created you to reach for the higher good. He created you to aspire to new levels. Something inside every single person, even a person incarcerated today who feels like they really messed up their life, says, "Wait. It's not over until it's over. I can be the person God wants me to be. I can change my old ways and become a brand-new person."

When you take the time to actually write virtues down, or memorize the faith acronym, and implement them every day, you're moving down a new trail, leading yourself in a new direction.

The Bible says, *"if anyone is in Christ, he is a new creation; the old has gone, the new has come!"* (2 Cor. 5:17). And remember Ephesians 4:23: *"be made new in the attitude of your minds."* The Bible talks about newness. The Bible talks about change. The Bible talks about transformation, and I think many people get the idea that it's a passive thing, that it's all up to God. What I want to help you understand today is that you must partner with God. You must decide, "What kind of person do I really want to be?" and then accomplish it.

You must partner with God.

Would you like to change your life and your future to be the best life you can live? You can! With faith and the P4-8 standard (and a rubber band, if needed), you can recognize, reject, and replace mind monsters that steal your life. You can retrain your mind to automatically think a new, better way; you can decide and say who you want to become, and keep a fresh mental attitude by incorporating God's thoughts into your daily routine.

You can become the person you want to be!

ABOUT THE AUTHOR

Kevin Gerald is most known for his communication of practical biblical principles that empower people to live successful Christian lives. He is the founder and senior pastor of Champions Centre, one of the largest congregations in the Pacific Northwest. Thousands are exposed to his relevant teaching of the Bible through his local and international television program, "Building Champions For Life."

Kevin and his wife, Sheila, reside in Puyallup, Washington, with their daughter, Jodi.

Access to Pastor Kevin Gerald's books and teaching materials can be found at www.kevingerald.com.

OTHER BOOKS BY KEVIN GERALD

Forces That Form Your Future
Developing Confidence
The Proving Ground
Raising Champion Children
Pardon Me, I'm Prospering
Characteristics of a Winner

Author Contact Information

Kevin Gerald Communications
c/o Champions Centre
1819 East 72nd Street
Tacoma, WA 98404

www.kevingerald.com